Note to parents, carers and teachers

Read it yourself is a series of modern stories, favourite characters, traditional tales and first reference books written in a simple way for children who are learning to read. The books can be read independently or as part of a guided reading session.

Each book is carefully structured to include many high-frequency words vital for first reading. The sentences on each page are supported closely by pictures to help with understanding, and to offer lively details to talk about.

The books are graded into levels that progressively introduce wider vocabulary and longer text as a reader's ability and confidence grow.

Ideas for use

- Although your child will now be progressing towards silent, independent reading, let him know that your help and encouragement is always available.

- Developing readers can be concentrating so hard on the words that they sometimes don't fully grasp the meaning of what they're reading. Answering the questions at the end of the book will help with understanding.

For more information and advice on
Read it yourself and book banding, visit
www.ladybird.com/readityourself

Book
Band
10

Level 4 is ideal for children who are ready to read longer texts with a wider vocabulary and who are eager to start reading independently.

Special features:

Richer, more varied vocabulary

Full exploration of subject

Detailed illustrations capture the imagination

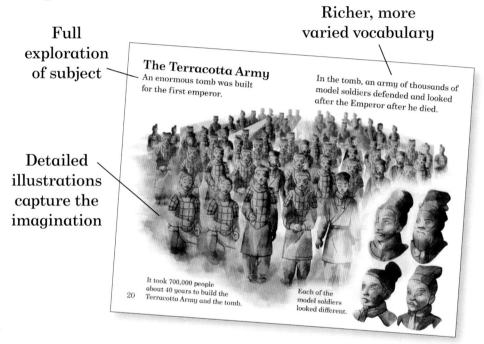

The Terracotta Army
An enormous tomb was built for the first emperor.

In the tomb, an army of thousands of model soldiers defended and looked after the Emperor after he died.

It took 700,000 people about 40 years to build the Terracotta Army and the tomb.

20

Each of the model soldiers looked different.

Longer sentences

Captions offer further explanation

Making paper
Paper was invented in China in about 100 CE. The first paper was made from tree bark.

4. A paper-making screen is put into the pulp.

screen

How paper was made

1. Tree bark is cut.

5. The pulp dries on the screen to become paper.

2. The bark is put in water.

6. The dry paper comes off the screen.

3. The bark becomes a pulp.

pulp

24

25

Educational Consultant: Geraldine Taylor
Book Banding Consultant: Kate Ruttle
Subject Consultant: Philip Parker

LADYBIRD BOOKS

UK | USA | Canada | Ireland | Australia
India | New Zealand | South Africa

Ladybird Books is part of the Penguin Random House group of companies
whose addresses can be found at global.penguinrandomhouse.com.

www.penguin.co.uk   www.puffin.co.uk   www.ladybird.co.uk

First published 2018
This edition 2019
002

Copyright © Ladybird Books Ltd, 2018

Printed in China

A CIP catalogue record for this book is available from the British Library

ISBN: 978-0-241-40540-6

All correspondence to:
Ladybird Books
Penguin Random House Children's
One Embassy Gardens, 8 Viaduct Gardens, London SW11 7BW

Ancient and Imperial China

Written by Simon Mugford

Illustrated by Leesh Li

Contents

Timeline

This is the timeline of ancient and imperial China.

221 BCE
The first emperor

475–221 BCE
Warring States

214 BCE
Emperor Qin
Shi Huang-di's
Great Wall

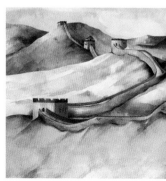

206 BCE–220 CE
Han Dynasty
*(Confucius's ideas
were important here)*

1912 CE
The last emperor

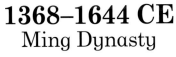

1368–1644 CE
Ming Dynasty

9

Warring States

Different family dynasties had ruled China as separate states for thousands of years. From about 475 BCE until 221 BCE, these states had many wars with each other.

This was the time of the Warring States in ancient China.

The first emperor

The ruler of the Qin kingdom was very powerful. After many wars, he ruled the separate states as one kingdom and became the first emperor.

Emperor Qin Shi Huang-di

Imperial China lasted for 2,000 years.

Emperor Qin Shi Huang-di was the first emperor of China. He ruled in the Qin Dynasty.

Different dynasties

China was ruled by different dynasties at different times.

Qin Dynasty

Emperor Qin Shi Huang-di's dynasty was the first to rule over all of ancient China.

Han Dynasty

The rulers of the
Han Dynasty made
imperial China
very powerful.

Han Dynasty
soldiers

Ming Dynasty

Chinese education and ideas
became more important in
this time.

The Great Wall

The different Chinese states built enormous walls to defend their kingdoms. Qin Shi Huang-di built one of the biggest walls, and joined other, older walls together, too.

The Great Wall of China

Most of the Great Wall we see today was built by the Ming Dynasty (1368–1644 CE).

Building the wall

Emperor Qin had thousands of soldiers and workers to build the wall for him.

Work on the Great Wall was done on and off for more than 1,500 years. The work was very hard.

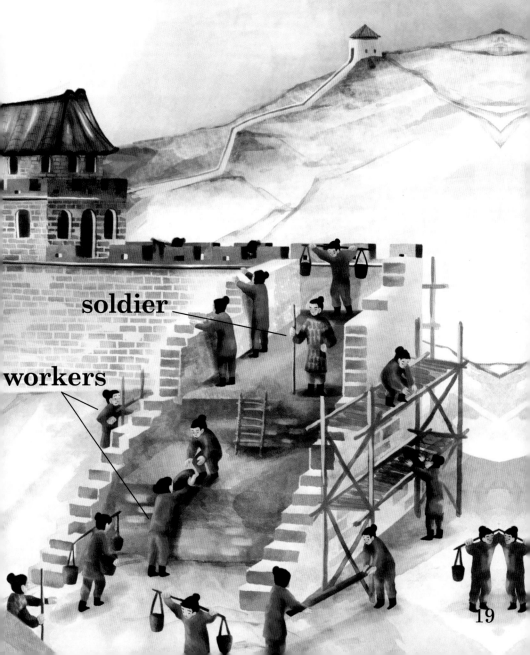

soldier

workers

The Terracotta Army

An enormous tomb was built
for the first emperor.

It took 700,000 people
about 40 years to build the
Terracotta Army and the tomb.

In the tomb, an army of thousands of model soldiers defended and looked after the Emperor after he died.

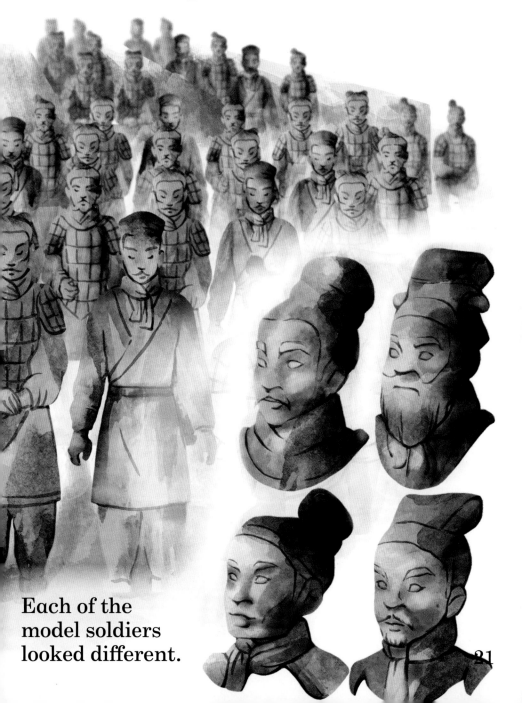

Each of the model soldiers looked different.

The great inventors

Many things that we still have today were invented in China. Silk, porcelain, fireworks, paper, printing and the compass are all Chinese inventions, and there are many more.

silk

porcelain

fireworks

paper

printing

compass

Making paper

Paper was invented in China in about 100 CE. The first paper was made from tree bark.

How paper was made

1. Tree bark is cut.

2. The bark is put in water.

3. The bark becomes a pulp.

pulp

4. A paper-making screen is put into the pulp.

screen

5. The pulp dries on the screen to become paper.

6. The dry paper comes off the screen.

Printing and power

As the rulers in China had more printed books, they became more educated and had good ideas. With more educated rulers, China became more powerful.

The world's first book was printed in China in 868 CE.

27

Chinese porcelain

The Chinese made the best porcelain in the world. The very best Chinese porcelain was made in the time of the Ming Dynasty.

Making Ming porcelain

Porcelain like this has another name: "china"!

28

Chinese medicine

The Chinese have used herbs in medicine for over 4,000 years. They invented acupuncture, too. In acupuncture, needles are used to treat illness.

herbs

Chinese medicine
and herbs are
still used to treat
illness today.

acupuncture
needles

The Silk Road

The ancient Chinese were great traders. From about 200 BCE, they were trading silk and other goods with people to the west. The way the traders went was called the "Silk Road".

The Silk Road brought new ideas from China to the west, too.

33

The ideas of Confucius

Confucius was a man who lived before the time of the Warring States. He said that family was very important, and that people should treat each other well.

Confucius's ideas helped
build a great Chinese
civilization during the
Han Dynasty.

35

Family life

In most Chinese families, mum, dad, children and grandparents all lived together.

Family life had rules.
The grandparents were the
most important people in the
family, and were looked up
to by children
and others.

37

Farming

Most people in ancient and imperial China lived by farming for food. The most important food in China was rice.

Families worked together on farms. Rice is still farmed in water, like this.

Chinese New Year

Chinese New Year has been celebrated for thousands of years. Today, it is an important time of year for Chinese people all over the world. Families come together to celebrate with food and fireworks.

People celebrate Chinese
New Year with fireworks!

China today

China is still a powerful and important country today, and Chinese goods are traded all over the world.

There are more people living in China than in any other country in the world.

43

Picture glossary

 compass

 emperor

 fireworks

 Great Wall of China

 medicine

 paper

 porcelain

 printing

 rice farm

 soldiers

 Terracotta Army

 tree bark

Index

Ancient and Imperial China quiz

What have you learnt about ancient and imperial China? Answer these questions and find out!

- What happened in China from about 475 BCE until 221 BCE?

- Who was the first emperor of China?

- What did Chinese states build to defend their kingdoms?

- Name one Chinese invention.

- Who was Confucius?

- How do people celebrate Chinese New Year?

www.ladybird.com